A Wellness Check

poems by

Bri Gonzalez

A Wellness Check

Copyright © 2024 by Bri Gonzalez

ISBN: 979-8-9899400-0-4

All rights reserved. No portion of this book may be
reproduced in any form without permission from
the publisher, except as permitted by U.S. copyright law.

Cover design and layout by Dave Mahan.

Edited by Ally Ang and Josh Savory.

www.gameoverbooks.com

8	Introducing the Rat
9	Ratman Meets Me in an Alleyway
10	Ratman Celebrates the Holidays
11	"For your dying pleasure, we are serving the very same acid that made us [who] we are today."
12	*Mad Love* (1993 & 1995)
13	A Wellness Check
24	Hypomanic? Absolutely. But Oh, So Divine!
25	Ratman Monitors My Blood Testing
26	< ? >
27	On Being in Love with the Clown Princess of Crime
28	Bipolar Support Group, Part One
31	In Which I (Finally) Am Not Real
32	Yassified Salt Lamp
33	Sleep Is Something We Fear
34	Ratman and I Refill Prescriptions at Your Local CVS
35	Dual-Form Insanity (You're Already Thinking, How Much More Is There to Say?)
36	People with Bipolar Disorder May Have Trouble Sleeping
37	I'm Not Trying to be Much of a Person Right Now
38	The Two-Faces of Bipolar
39	Ratman Streams My Diagnosis on Netflix
40	https://www.youtube.com/watch?v=1B-L4xLWaUQ
41	< ? >
42	How to Commit Someone in Four Parts
43	Rogues Gallery
44	Dear AMC President, Nicole Kidman
51	< ¿ >
52	Ratman Meets Me in an Alleyway
53	Someone on Season Five of *Halloween Baking Championship* Is Making a Pumpkin Pie Inspired by Dr. Jekyll and Mr. Hyde
54	Happy Days/Get Happy
55	Ode to Ammit (i.e., Please Devour Me)

56	Midsommar (2019)
57	to bruce / to my future / bruce
60	Bipolar Support Group, Part Two
61	Sitting at a Table with Rahul Kohli and Shira Erlichman
62	Steven Grant and I Commiserate Over Our Respective Brain Functions
63	Manic and/or Semi-Sentient
65	Ode to Travis Willingham
67	"Great film! Really drew me in. The crazy girl had a few different things woven together to create an experience in the viewer."
69	Ratman Prescribes Me 200 MG Lamictal
70	There's a Speech Bubble Over My Head Saying, "Twice as Ill, Twice as Dangerous!"
71	Bipolar Support Group, Part ?
73	What Some Might Define as Reverse Psychology
74	Ratman Meets Me in an Alleyway
75	Is This What You Mean by Journaling?
77	I Dream of Multiverses Without Madness
79	Bipolar Support Group, Archived
83	Notes
85	Acknowledgements
86	Gratitudes
88	Biography

For YOU!

Introducing the Rat

He could scamper for the neck—
taut, exposed, vein-ribbed, fresh.
But he's not interested in curved
yearning, muscle-stretch canvas,
snapping a free palm.

Instead, he darts for the skull.
Smudge-eyed snarl. A blood
glove. He shouldn't be able
to. Squeaks his way in and
chews up cerebellum,
whips matter into metal ladders.
Nibbles—a death reveal.

Snatched in his maw, he
shadow-delivers, part-
carcass, part-cranium, cracked.
Slumped in a side street.

Ratman Meets Me in an Alleyway

and it's a wellness check. Wouldn't let the City Police get their organized/crimed hands on me. He scoops, surrenders me to his hip like an infant, tangles my hair on his cowl. Can't turn his head to check but I'm staining his ratsuit, I'm crying blood and chalk, I'm drawing houses on his shoulder blades. Here is the most accurate image—raw nails, finger printing. He says shh once then twice more. He locks me with my people. He stops himself from punching my face. I shine a light out my window, rat-taped bulb, and he grips and bars. Tells me he's sorry.

Ratman Celebrates the Holidays

by going to his victims' cells. Chrome-wrapped, leather-bowed, Santa hat roosted on his rat tail. He forces gifts through our foot slats, handing out apologies:

- ~~Señor Arctic: hand-knit scarf~~
- ~~Flytrap: rubber succulent~~
- ~~Quippler: nine hundred and ninety-nine puzzle pieces (out of a thousand)~~
- ~~Mr. Double-Side: Mederma skin care gel for scars, acne, stretch marks, etc.~~
- Me: orange plastic, overflowing, abundant
    - i.e., a throat forced open

He promises to be back for New Years.

"For your dying pleasure, we are serving the very same acid that made us [who] we are today."

Mr. Double-Side and I have matching needles
in our bloodstreams. When we walk, we jingle,
eyes threaded with cells and sinew.

Sometimes our bodies pop and we upset.

Double-Side fishes one out, teaches me
how to sew. Being science
experiments, we place our needles
on chairs or tires.

Sometimes we unhinge; our mouthed,
clotted thread—tangled, pooling faces.

Doctors/cops/people (Ratman)
trail us, press tubes to us.
Collect sticks of chalk
and stray wrists.
Pinch a loose stab.

Double-Side hands me
a trigger. I offer him
my cheek.

Mad Love (1993 & 1995)

She unleashes herself

when she's ready.
She clutters your belly
with macerated midbrain,
guiding mush into

splotchy puncture sites. She nips
you woozy, scavenges your

calcium before climaxing.
I think you might

be lucky enough. Once she
greases each corner and crease,
she stenches. Compounds the wet
of her itch until you're both

garbage bags brimming with rot.
Outside the window, a howling

full moon psychosis. She
knots us before your judgment.
She dumps me needy.
Polyethylene and limp,

inside me a god.

A Wellness Check
after Lily Hoang

Ratman hangs his cape in the front closet while I microwave a second bowl of oatmeal, and we cozy on the couch, his bulk protruding from the arm and edge. I put on *Little Miss Sunshine*, tell Ratman how I want to watch all of Paul Dano's films before I die, which might be soon. He nods between slopped spoonfuls. He swaddles me, constructs a fortress of Hello Kitty Squishmallows. After the movie is over, he admits he's taking me on a grippy sock detour.

///

A counselor sighs at fourth-grade me. Life is sad is her wisdom. She needs to know if everything is okay at home.

///

"Aren't you being a little dramatic?" Ratman asks.

///

The day I was born, my mother flipped a coin.
What came out: splinter-surfaced scream, hot pink
fuzz, a two-toned baby suit and torn
lips. She keeps asking if there's a cure.

///

Some dot edu text declares bipolar to be possibly born from childhood trauma. I don't believe it at first but think of all the times my aunt was the wife who cried wolf and my uncle the lycanthrope we silver-bulleted. I still don't believe it, but I cry about being more

///

I text Jesse pictures of my Barnes & Noble shopping spree. She wants to know how much it cost. She suggests my purchase is *so manic of me*, that I should tell Dr. Ratman.

///

"You really don't seem like you have that at all."

///

My brother doesn't want me taking lithium.
                                                        It's too dangerous, too harmful,
too likely to blacken my kidneys without a second chance.
                              My brother suggests
I seek out non-drug treatments.
He reminds me I was diagnosed with bipolar   not that long ago.

///

"You're out of your mind... You're sick... You're going to die alone..." – [Ratman] to the [Quippler], in *The [Ratman]* (2022)

///

The Quippler and I are having an affair. We spitball love letters across the hallway.

///

Everyone insists the   is dangerous. No, no, look. It tamps down the supervillain in me. Prevents me from becoming another nemesis for Ratman to suckerpunch. They say hospitals are for the weak and I say yes, I am, and kick my head back.

///

Mr. Double-Side only speaks about love in death
       and I think he's onto something.
What the fuck is going on with me?

///

Anubis weighs the heart of every deceased individual. If a heart weighs less than a feather, a person's soul is committed to whatever comes next. However, if it's found heavy, demoness Ammit will swallow them whole. Will be their end.

///

Ratman's mother/aunt/father/cousin/uncle used to be where I am.
I'm not supposed to know this.

///

My sister continues to emphasize that I can stop medication whenever I like.

///

Is it serious? My sister eyes the clean divide of me. *Is it anything serious?*

///

No one believes me when I say I'm demisexual. I am the ruler of smash or pass, fuck marry kill, unleashing the vibrator every night, each shift of the moon witness to the rocketlaunch of myself. Two peach pills not enough to shackle my superpower. My ability to be an ouroboros of pleasure. Only when I splinter from the libido-high do people listen. By then, I am too exhausted to talk.

///

Before Ratman was Ratman he was a rat king and before that
he was a PhD student studying clinical psychology.

///

Snapchat Memories says hey here's some evidence you've always been a parabola. It's bizarre, the frame-by-frame breakdown of a y-axis. I wish I could invent pixelated time travel just to warn myself. Instead, I relive one a.m. ramblings and need to lie on the floor for a while. I don't have the means to express the weight of swallowing permanence.

///

I masturbate to the Ratmobile for two weeks straight.

///

During visiting hours, I introduce my brother to Mr. Double-Side, and they shake hands.

///

Ratman gets me a day out of Asylum. He takes me
to an alleyway and describes how coping mechanisms
are my best friend. He punches me bricked. He hammers
down, dismantles the fire escape, reigns knuckles until I'm
burst and brittle red.

///

Sleep cry. No cry with/out sleep. No sleep, no cry.
Do you understand?

///

Located in G. City, Asylum is where Ratman's foes who are mentally ill are brought as patients.

(Other foes are incarcerated at Penitentiary).

///

Ratman is the sunbaby from *The Teletubbies*. Let's rescind this far back into our inner child.

///

"–those who are considered to no longer be mentally unwell tend to re-offend."

///

My brother can't fathom layered fear.
Why I don't want kids.

///

"Amadeus decided, as sole heir to the… estate… remodeled his family home to treat the mentally ill, so others might not suffer his mother's fate."

///

There is no harmless. I am diagnosed.

///

Or: there is no diagnosed. I am harmless.

///

"… too psychologically paralyzing for anyone to thrive?"

///

The Rat Signal is on, which means he'll visit tonight. He's on the hunt for a roommate. I like being padlocked alone, but he won't listen. Can't hear through the cowl. He despises how much time I spend with Clown Princess and Quippler and Mr. Double-Side. I ask, if he hates it so much,

why does he lock me up? We both know. He grapplehooks away, empty-fisted.

///

"What is it about the wrong kind of men?" – Nicole Kidman in *[Ratman] Forever*

///

Sometimes I know exactly what gods feel like and it's not sacred or glorious or holy.

///

The Mother of All Quips.
How did I end up like this?

///

Dr. Ratman tells me I have lived many lives.
Beyond my years.
So full of age.

///

We think. He's the source.

///

Two cigarettes per seam. A split chair. We.

///

I've seen ten Paul Dano films and I won't make it in time.

///

Stopped clock.

///

My brother frowns.
All your smoking will kill
you. An earthly death.
I ask how earthly.

///

Señor Arctic offers cryogenics. It's not the same.

///

My aunt insists my cousin obtain a psych eval if he wants to live at home because she needs to know how deep the infection dances.

///

I'm always saying,
"There is no fix. I don't want one. I am the way."

///

Another day of Dr. Ratman raining down on Quippler and Flytrap and Mr. Double-Side. Another day of witnessing, wondering how exactly I fit into place. Another day of walking to the lab so they can draw me out, spin me around, determine if my thyroid still has any value. In the infirmary, my inmates are stitched up and iced out and I am clamping the tenderness between my forearm and bicep, buds of purple-yellow settling themselves into my moles. Dr. Ratman offers to kiss it better in my next session before asking on a scale of one to five how often I've felt hopeless in the last two weeks.

///

I text my friend Jesse that I'm in a hypomanic state. She replies, *Sucks dude.*

///

Dr. Ratman recommends mindfulness. Guided breathing might mend me.

///

My roommate hums indifferently as I explain the step-by-step process of starting Lamictal.

"You have to build doses in small increments every two weeks. So, fifty milligrams for fourteen days, then a hundred, then one-fifty. If you up the amount too quickly, a lethal rash could break out."

Uh-huh.

I want to respond: "Which is to say if I chug too many of these dust pellets, throbbing poison boils will overtake my flesh, a coup eventually spreading to the nervous system. The lead boil, a boil dictator, will shut down all previous bodily administrations. Before the boils win, I'll attempt to pop them, a smattering of acid. I'll die a cautionary tale. Beware the boil insurgence. Beware the physiopolitical conflicts of sickness."

I ask how her week is going.

///

Dr. Ratman always says I hear you, and I'm pretty sure he's lying.

///

A skinned threat.

///

Steph says illness is a rite of passage. Everyone goes in solid and comes out crunched and I should stop making a big deal.

///

Late Middle English: via late Latin from Greek, literally 'madness,' from mainesthai: 'be mad.'

///

Anthony Padilla's video, "I spent a day with people w/ BIPOLAR DISORDER," is sponsored by HelloFresh.

///

I make the call. That call. I'm holding half an hour.

///

Ratman as a label maker. Slapping on names and phrases and pills and justifications for pummeling, sinking rat mouth, clawing out eyes and ending up the hero. Sick in the head is to irreparable, violent evil. He scurries around sticking label on label on label. Crossing the street with my mother, I point to his cape flourish, and say there's your proof. There is no saving.

///

Everyone in Asylum wants to fuck Ratman.

///

My friend Ashton decides that Clown Princess is bipolar.
I scream in his face until each tooth pops out, handfuls of chalk capsules.

///

"I'm having a breakthrough. And a breakdown? Maybe!" – Jim Carrey as the [Quippler] in [Ratman] Forever

///

Today, Dr. Ratman stalks up to the bars. He loops his hands in, gloves me close. He presses his lips between the gaps and doesn't retreat for ten minutes.

///

Adopting a cat wasn't intended to be a suicide prevention strategy but she's working.

///

Ratman asks if I miss you, has shitty bedside manner.

///

"Ever since graduation, I've been feeling so low—I mean not like your condition, but y'know—"

///

If I have to lose half my face, fingers crossed it's not the side with my nose ring.

///

If my great-aunt were still around, she'd remind me mental illness isn't real because she never felt it. She'd cup my hand around a dove folded from her favorite proverb. It's as simple as praying it away. God will protect your soul if you're worthy. Alright, I'll give it a shot. I shut my eyes and radiate thoughts of forgiveness and shelter. God is not the answering savior. My great-aunt, head bowed, beads a crucifix behind my ear and opens the front door. Dr. Ratman, my only salvation, thanks my aunt for her efforts.

Hypomanic? Absolutely. But Oh, So Divine![1]

Before I transform into all you expect,
let's enjoy ourselves. Scavenge cigarette
ghosts, investigate the abandoned
abandoned, crumble new offerings
of chaos across county lines. Kidnap four-
leaf clovers, reinvent mistletoe's reputation.

Let's pretend our battered Honda Civics
are battleships. Let's indulge the whispering.
If you feel your stomach twine, remember, I'm

the scariest thing here.
As in: There are benefits to destruction.
Every smile a consequence I'm required to fix.
I want to know, what about looped doom?
What more besides waiting for my crash?

We're coloring elbow bruises.
You ask how it feels

to see a godly pour in me. We knot
friendship bracelets until dusk,
until you slink away, avoiding
my lithiumed invocation.

---

[1] Quippler spots me in the *New York Times*, next to the crosswords. He tries to solve me but gives up, scratches out my title and renames me the Mother of All Quips. My grandiosity begs for tragedy. The paper clears its throat. Reads itself aloud. *Mania can inspire desolation sprees but can also generate. You know? Oh, you manic depressive. Devour your effusiveness and then paralyze despair. It's laughable, how easy it is to lose your balance.*

Ratman Monitors My Blood Testing

Lithium is a chemical element that sits
stainless in my belly stubs raw where throat
is edged into sickness rubs carbonate is
a concrete flesh is synthetical is something
you know about poke my pucker
mineral uppercut there's a full bottle
clacking can you please ask if it wants
a cup of potassium without breaking all
the orchids in the sink

< ? >

how do i
how do i
how do i
how do i
how do i
how do i
who do i
how why i
how do i
      and if i
what do i
      and if i
when do i
      and if i
when do i
      and if i will i
      and if i will i
      and if i will i
          will i when
          will i when
          will i when
          will i when
             when
             when
                how
             when
                how long
             when
                how long will   will it
                how long

                              you have to consume me

                              do you know what i

On Being in Love with the Clown Princess of Crime

Histrionic Personality Disorder is defined
by the American Psychiatric Association
as a pattern of excessive attention-seeking,
including inappropriate seduction and excessive desire for approval.

Clown Princess raises the issue of me being her inverse, committed to Dr. Ratman.
She says I deserve better.
We paint each other's nails through bars—buckled arms and tooth-gripped patience.

Treatment may include antipsychotics, such as
aripiprazole/abilify/aristada/olanzapine/zyprexa/quetiapine/seroquel/
risperidone/risperdal.

She lets her crazy out. I swallow. Unsheathe glitter bristles and lip the side of her.

People with Schizotypal Personality Disorder have odd behavior,
speech patterns, thoughts, and perceptions. Other people often describe
them as strange, eccentric. Suspicious. Paranoid.

After the night guards patrol my block, I conjure Princess in my room.
We sketch houses together. She box-dyes my blue. I don't know if I want
her or to be her. She thwacks her mallet on my chest again and again
until I make that face. I reverse, say she deserves better. We rattle through
the night. My doctor, you know the one, says you can't keep a good
weirdo down.

If depressive symptoms are severe and medication is not effective,
    ECT may be used.

Bipolar Support Group, Part One

YOU and MR. DOUBLE-SIDE are seated at The Diner. RATMAN emerges from the rat shadows.

              DOUBLE-SIDE:
      It's not about what I want.
      It's about the houses beneath.
      I know you can see them.

DOUBLE-SIDE extends his arms. They wriggle like earthworms under a recently-watered stone. The WAITRESS and RATMAN nod.

              DS:
We thought we could be decent. We could bend to the rules without crumbling. I opened a therapy app that said, "Hey, here's a mountain. It's your mountain."

      (DOUBLE-SIDE looks to YOU).

The city spits us out like a smattering of acid and we bear the force of it. (The vinyl booth creaks beneath DOUBLE-SIDE as he slurps his coffee. YOU do the same. Your mouths are linked).

There are two options in a place that violences us. One: we chew. Two: we pinprick. Neither are good options but it's all we have. Isn't it?

YOU nod.

              RATMAN:
Okay but have you tried breathing? Or maybe walking on the sun for a while?

YOU and DOUBLE-SIDE crack jaws. Out pours winterbourne needles clattering on the booth like miniature wind chimes. The WAITRESS and RATMAN retreat to avoid sickening their respective (rat) suits.

                    RATMAN:
Don't make an appointment if you have nothing to talk about, it's a disrespect to my time. If it's really an emergency, you know what number to dial, remember?

YOU and DOUBLE-SIDE motion to cleaved cheeks. You're suffering.

                    DS/YOU (simult.):
We've scribbled a thousand iterations. We've powdered our throats, offered blood and beakered ourselves in return. There's a reader who flip / flips us. We're tired. Fighting to remain awake. Exactly how soon do you expect us to process? Please, let us eat our pie.

                    RATMAN (to YOU):
You, you were supposed to be the best of us. I see you; I hear you.

You are listening, the wheels in your deranged mind sticking.

                    RATMAN (again, to YOU):
You're not alone/Your story isn't over/I care/ There is hope.

RATMAN begins speaking so rapidly, his bootlaces unknot, and he wobbles, tripping over himself.

> RATMAN:
> I've typed all this in a colorful font on a laminated poster. Here's an aromatherapy candle. (It smells like cedarwood and orange.) Everyone feels whatever it is you're feeling sometimes/ You'll be okay.

RATMAN inches your way. YOU and DOUBLE-SIDE cry. They do not let YOU keep the candle in Asylum.

In Which I (Finally) Am Not Real

At the time   it made

    classic   illness in the   world

        a classic reexamination
                proposing

manifestations   a deeper   whole

    impairment,

a spotlight on   the concept

    its purpose   failed to
                         exist

              psychotic
    automatically transforms
                  even though it is
extremely unreliable

        as a disease entity

                    they

    enjoy their brief

lowering   number of days

Yassified Salt Lamp

It's not all bad all the time.
My friend Ada visits, plays Uno
with me and Señor Arctic,
reminds me I have options.

Double down on the sickness they say,
sprinkle it in my coffee or toothpaste,
stomach the bittersour. Or, they offer, scamper
to sickness, sin in the skull, spill it on the floor
with Dr. Ratman's lips, with my family's insistence
I'm a late-bloom changeling ("You're not really you.")
Lastly, they suggest, pay the sickness no mind.

I sneak Ada into my cell so we can photoshop
acrylic nails and false eyelashes onto a salt lamp.
We swipe our tongues up and down my forearms,
recoiling then laughing at the strike of mineral.

Sleep Is Something We Fear

You look into a mirror and there
are two more of you. They are not
kind. They sneer, dizzy-bark, call
you a rat without a tail. They beg to
batter your brain in inverted grips.
Thoth is the Egyptian god of the mind
you lack. Your doubles relay this to you.
When you try to compass, their words
are backwards and you're in bed, wrists
velcro-cinched. Your feet are sand,
your tongue is dead, you do not
understand, and you spiral.
They are not kind.
They call you a rat without a tail.

Set murders Osiris:
he tricks his brother into fourteen
pieces and treasure-hunts him.
Your doubles relay this to you.
Something is trying to put you to sleep.
You look into a mirror and there is
one of you.

Ratman and I Refill Prescriptions at Your Local CVS[2]

teethfull pills pilled teeth teethed milligrams
power residue molar measuring tongue
balances canine cratering lungs dryswallow
most don't too many teeththroated
teethbitter bliss tastebuds tastedrawn
blooddrawn maps veins pinpoints places
to beg and Ratman teeths off each one

---

[2] Ratman pins me against the wall, thumbs my gums, whispers pick-up lines to my esophagus. Paw on waist and all. Is it trashy to think about kissing him? It's the beady eyes. It's the way he's set on curing me. It's the eye roll he suppresses when I mention my soul dipping into the shadow realm. *Do it*, I mantra. *Do it do it doitdoitdoit*. Dr. Ratman is not that kind of psychiatrist/vigilante.

Dual-Form Insanity (You're Already Thinking, How Much More Is There to Say?)

once upon a time there was a once upon a time once upon a once time there
upon a brain chose to be full of maggots once maggots chose to be a colony
of hands upon sulci gyri upon play-doh reorganized synapse time once a brain
mold of neon jello once upon a smattering of acid once a child sleep declined
cried a time once child refused fluid once again time adult-child upon moving
navigated tissue burns once bodies are in the nature of sabotage in time
none of this matters once none of this matters once upon a time
there was Ratman who cuffed my wrists to salvage them so many times
i am a danger to myself

People with Bipolar Disorder May Have Trouble Sleeping

The Quippler is standing beside my bed while I sleep. He wafts back and forth, a ghost uncertain, before crawling in. I have giant wings, leathered and scarred, and no face. He kisses my blankness through his mask. Underneath his mask is

another mask. Underneath my nothing is flesh and bone, outlet-less mouth. I ask for water and the Quippler lifts an orange cup. He spills capsules, each one dissolving into my skin. He's sorry one too many times. Tries to f/suck them out. I wake a shadow

past my door frame. I wake and the Quippler shakes me. Beneath his mask is Ratman, whimpering. I wake again. My cat beggars for breakfast. The fan whirs bony bird chirps. Sun dismantles purple dawn and my alarm cycles. I find I have wet the bed.

I'm Not Trying to be Much of a Person Right Now

by fetaling on the ground and bingeing *Cupcake Wars*. If I focus enough, I become the ground-beef-chocolate-gravy-topped cupcake pasted between Florian Bellanger's molars, worming my way up to his gum line where I hibernate until his six-month dental work reminder. Or, I'll clog his throat, and Justin Willman will have to man up and unearth the plunger cobwebbed behind the leftmost oven, stashed there for this exact reason. When Justin isn't strong enough to rubber me deep, Ratman will step in, snake a spined gauntlet past Bellanger's French. He drags me back to Asylum. A sedative named quetiapine fumarate surrenders itself to peach puddles. It is lonely. It yearns to be bodied, absorbed, and dissipated into semi-non-existence, which I can empathize with. "What are you doing here, Ratman? What are you doing?" From the studio exit, I see Candace Nelson flicked on the Rat Signal. Her smile clumps of rainbow sprinkles. Sometimes, rather than becoming a cupcake, I stare out the window until I pane. Two doors down, someone blares Mitski and yodels about a girl who eats asphalt, refusing to become a puzzle. I want to die and no one cares. Or, I want to die and everyone cares. Or, I want to die and everyone cares except me. Or, we all want to die but I insist on being the main character. My brother texts me, orders me to be a person. The moon tells me she/he/they love me, but I'm not convinced. Did I tell you I want to die? It's nothing special.

The Two-Faces of Bipolar

I post gradient-shaded statistics on Instagram
because it's the only way I can be more
than Ratman's side-bitch in a straitjacket.

Even then, there are other things to double-tap,
like rats managing a Starbucks storefront or
a lingerie company specialized in sebum panty sets
or the gender reveal of your high school bully,
fingers crossed her child is pug-ugly and un-special.

I don't delete my account like Ratman insists.
It's like coming out all over again, minus
the guarantees I am still loved.

My family members' comments vary
between "you are just Ratman's side-bitch
in a straitjacket" and "wow, you are *so brave*"
and "this post is too much to read" and "hey did you
see that video of rats managing a Starbucks?"

Ratman Streams My Diagnosis on Netflix

horror movie where I am killer // victim
                          crooked :: survival

I am axe-wielder ::
    hockey-costumed-blank-
    faced-clown-masked-shape
                    forest bulk
  weapon gore-ached //

I am lover-turned-
      murderer // mother
        post-retribution // crazed
                fan bent on breaking //
snapped straitjacket
        huddle :: mirror shards ::
                spiral eye descent ::

I am
    broken-down bus // escaped
    asylum inmate // pill-devourer ::
                jump-scare

I am skin bones :: you fear
  a brained-violence
  existing // threat ::

I am swing-pierced back ::
    hacked and cracked
    down // my evil
  self-baptized
  crimson //

  I   split until my body ::

    shattered flesh-kissed piles of death

https://www.youtube.com/watch?v=1B-L4xLWaUQ

Passing lips slip pacified
until tongue cradles smooth, chin-
dropped hesitations, anxious teeth
unwilling to shut tumbled skin—
jawbroke abductions; desperate,
muffled meditations; your fingers;
cheek molting; dimlighted
clench and semi-collapse;
maw fizzed spit. I lollipop the map
of your hands—
cherished blessings throw bones
out the church door.
Our cavities waltz.

< ? >

Quetiapine fumarate is an antipsychotic.

I dream a tarot reading.
Every card is the Hanged Man.

They say I need to build a house.
I flip / flip and they repeat: I need
to build a house I want to live in.

I start with spine. I start with texture.
I start with sharp angles on the floorboards.

I need to	/	build
build a	/	a brain
broken	/	door I want
to need	/	a house
I want	/	smattering
to live	/	in.

It's not working.
I wake to find I've wet the bed.

How to Commit Someone in Four Parts

as in: don't look at me
and expect function.

there is a dowry: ten-
thousand orange bottles
for you to store me in,
circled and obedient.
thumbelina with less guts.
pollypocket Rx.

fold me an origami key
with (de)construction
paper and seal each
cylinder tight. it's
make-or-break as i wedge
between plastic ridging.

this, your reward: i fit
easily into the average
medicine cabinet.

Rogues Gallery

Ratman whose foes   are mentally ill
Ratman whose foes   are mentally ill
Ratman whose foes   are mentally ill
Ratman whose foes   are mentally ill
Ratman whose foes   are mentally ill
Ratman whose foes   are mentally ill
Ratman whose foes   are mentally ill
Ratman whose foes   are mentally ill
Ratman whose foes   are mentally ill
Ratman whose foes   are mentally ill

once upon a smattering of acid
once upon a smattering of acid
once upon a smattering of acid
once upon a smattering of acid
once upon a smattering of acid   pinch a loose stab
once upon a smattering of acid   pinch a loose stab
I start with a pin   on a smattering of acid   pinch a loose stab
I start with a pin   on a smattering of acid   pinch a loose stab
I start with a pin   on a smattering of acid   pinch a loose stab

you're sick, you're going to die alone   pinch a loose stab
you're sick, you're going to die alone   I start with a pin   pinch a loose stab
you're sick, you're going to die alone   I start with a pin   quetiapine fumarate an antipsychotic
you're sick, you're going to die alone   I start with a pin   quetiapine fumarate an antipsychotic
you're sick, you're going to die alone   I start with a pin   quetiapine fumarate an antipsychotic   pinch a loose stab
you're sick, you're going to die alone   I start with a pin   quetiapine fumarate an antipsychotic   pinch a loose stab

quetiapine fumarate an antipsychotic
quetiapine fumarate an antipsychotic
quetiapine fumarate an antipsychotic   it seems you can't keep a good weirdo down
bodies are in the nature of sabotage   quetiapine fumarate an antipsychotic   it seems you can't keep a good weirdo down
bodies are in the nature of sabotage   quetiapine fumarate an antipsychotic   it seems you can't keep a good weirdo down
bodies are in the nature of sabotage   quetiapine fumarate an antipsychotic   it seems you can't keep a good weirdo down
bodies are in the nature of sabotage   quetiapine fumarate   you need to build a house you want to live in
wake to find bed wet   bodies are in the nature of sabotage   you need to build a house you want to live in
wake to find bed wet   bodies are in the nature of sabotage   you need to build a house you want to live in
wake to find bed wet   bodies are in the nature of sabotage   you need to build a house you want to live in
wake to find bed wet   bodies are in the nature of sabotage   you need to build a house you want to live in   too late
wake to find bed wet   bodies are in the nature of sabotage   you need to build a house you want to live in   too late
wake to find bed wet   Ratman asks if I miss you   too late
wake to find bed wet   Ratman asks if I miss you   too late
a wellness check and it's a wellness check   Ratman asks if I miss you   too late
a wellness check and it's a wellness check   Ratman asks if I miss you   too late
a wellness check and it's a wellness check   it's too late it's too late it's too late
a wellness check and it's a wellness check   it's too late it's too late it's too late
a wellness check and it's a wellness check   it's too late it's too late it's too late
a wellness check and it's a wellness check   it's too late it's too late it's too late
a wellness check and it's a wellness check   it's too late it's too late it's too late
                                               it's too late it's too late it's too late
                                               it's too late it's too late it's too late

Dear AMC President, Nicole Kidman

I'm selling the very tickets you perforate out of me. Screw loose capitalism, center of a Venn diagram, Asylum comic in my glove box. I park beneath the streetlamp I'm supposed to murder myself under. In theater three, someone has a mental breakdown and Dr. Ratman escorts them out. My coworker admits he wanted to see Ratman smash through his own standee and tackle the customer, beat them to a rat-fisted pulp. The benefit here is me stealing blue raspberry slushies as a form of self-medication. At least twenty times per shift, the lithium-brain kicks in, and I forget why I'm serving the industry that wants me sedated or dead. ABC dot net dot au lists the cause of spending during manic overload as simply a lack of inhibition. Welcome to a lifetime of chipping Señor Arctic away, freezer-burning fingernails to un-subzero my debit cards. I sneak the Ratman standee home, tuck him in bed with me. Does heartbreak feel good in a place like this? The hot dog roller offers to buy my groceries and I know what comes next. I quit after two weeks so Dr. Ratman can pursue more intensive treatment. I walk to my car.

I'm selling the   perforated   me
Screw loose   center of a
                  comic in my glove   I
beneath   Ratman
                        a rat-fisted pulp
                                    a form of self-
medication. I forget   I'm   the
                  sedated or dead. Welcome
to a   freezer
burning   .
I sneak   Ratman   home, tuck him in   me.
Does heartbreak feel good   like this?

Welcome to

                          Ratman
               in   me.

YOU'RE IN A LOBBY CHAIR NEXT TO A MINI ZEN GARDEN. TWENTY PAMPHLETS SHOOT SYMPATHY FROM ACROSS THE ROOM. THREE RATS WORK THE FRONT DESK, NIBBLING ON MOUSE CORDS. SOMEONE SAYS THE BRAIN IS LIKE BAMBOOZLED JELLY BEANS AND YOUR ARMS ARE RAGGED WITH MAPS. EACH MINUTE IS ACCOMPANIED BY VOMIT— CAFFEINE-FLECKED APRICOT JAM. THE DOCTOR HANDS YOU A FORM THAT SAYS HEY CAN YOU QUANTIFY HOW INTENSELY YOU FEEL YOUR CANINES WIGGLING OUT OF THEIR SOCKETS AND YOU SAY NO BUT IT ASKS AGAIN ANYWAYS. THE DOCTOR IS RATMAN, BROODING. AS YOU ANSWER THE FORM'S DEMANDS, YOUR FINGERS HARDEN INTO STICKS OF REDBLUEYELLOW DULLED CHALK THAT RASP FINE DUST, SKETCHING HOUSES ON DR. RATMAN'S CHEST. YOU WONDER HOW MUCH MORE OF THIS YOU CAN SWALLOW. THE FORM ADMITS HEY SORRY I NEED YOU TO ALSO RATE HOW OFTEN YOU CURL AROUND THE COFFEE TABLE MOTIONLESS UNTIL YOU BECOME A GHOST THAT YOUR FUTURE SELF CAN WALK THROUGH. AT YOUR LOCAL CVS, A RECEIPT BEGINS TO DO THE WORM.

THE SINK IS FLOODED WITH ORCHIDS.

DR. RATMAN POUNDS ON MR. DOUBLE-SIDE UNTIL THE CRATER OF HIM SLOUGHS OFF, PUDDLE OF PINK CELLOPHANE AND GAUZE. DR. RATMAN CALLS IT EXPOSURE THERAPY.

IT'S TOO LATE IT'S TOO LATE IT'S TOO LATE HE'S TOO LATE IT'S TOO LATE IT'S TOO LATE IT'S TOO LATE HE'S TOO LATE HE'S TOO HE'S LATE IT'S LATE I'M TOO LATE IT'S TOO MUCH TOO MUCH IT'S TOO MUCH TOO LATE HE'S SCOOPING ME HE'S TAKING ME HE'S TOO LATE I'M TOO MUCH IT'S

< ¿ >³

```
                          mis primos tios tías
                          mis primos tios tías
                          mis primos tios tías
                          mis primos tios tías
                          mis primos tios tías
                          mis primos tios tías
                          mis primos tios tías
                          mis primos tios tías
                          mis primos tios tías ¿somos siempre de esta patria?
                          mis primos tios tías ¿somos siempre de esta patria?
                          mis primos tios tías ¿somos siempre de esta patria?
                                               ¿somos siempre de esta patria?
                                               ¿somos siempre de esta patria?
                                               ¿somos siempre de esta patria?
          las ratas sin las colas las ratas sin las colas ¿somos siempre de esta patria?
          las ratas sin las colas las ratas sin las colas
          las ratas sin las colas las ratas sin las colas
          las ratas sin las colas las ratas sin las colas
          las ratas sin las colas las ratas sin las colas
          las ratas sin las colas las ratas sin las colas so much time you damage me well
          las ratas sin las colas las ratas sin las colas so much time you damage me well
                          so much time you damage me well
                          so much time you damage me well
                          so much time you damage me well
                          so much time you damage me well
                          so much time you damage me well
                          so much time you damage me well       la sal y la sal
uela besa mis manos como el viento so much time you damage me well la sal y la sal
uela besa mis manos como el viento so much time you damage me well la sal y la sal
uela besa mis manos como el viento so much time you damage me well la sal y la sal viéndome
uela besa mis manos como el viento lo veo lo veo la sal y la sal viéndome
                          lo veo lo veo la sal y la sal viéndome
                          lo veo lo veo la sal y la sal viéndome
                          lo veo lo veo la sal y la sal viéndome
                                        la sal y la sal
                                        la sal y la sal
                                        la sal y la sal
```

³ Ancestry.com offers me the knotted reality. Don't worry if you can't understand this, neither can I. My abuela tosses salt over her shoulder for protection and I go soaring, crashing. This side of my family refuses to avert their aversion. We point fingers without knowing why. A rat without a tail will not survive long due to lack of balance. Dr. Ratman proudly reminds me he's finished Unit One of Duolingo's Spanish course.

Ratman Meets Me in an Alleyway

Warns me—don't venture near their kind, he says,
stiff squinted crusade, rain-smitten.
He begs me to take my meds.

Fuck Ratman.
I dump my pills.

I sit at a diner booth with Quippler and
Mr. Double-Side. We order coffee and pie.

Double-Side cocoons me. Tears in our mugs bloom
like swelling creamer. I kiss his tissue-mottled
cheek before velcroing off my own.
We wait for glass-booted bursting.

The Rat is disappointed.

I shake my fist, Asylum bound.

Someone on Season Five of *Halloween Baking Championship* Is Making a Pumpkin Pie Inspired by Dr. Jekyll and Mr. Hyde[4]

with dulce de leche and Mexican hot chocolate. Can't you see my portrait here? The non-camera-touched pie parts are cleaved in two
by crew members, then hurled at a rusting dumpster. Producers ensure each seed is splintered and burnt.
Mr. Double-Side, is this why we're at the diner together?
Ordering more of ourselves?

---

[4] In case you were wondering, the baker went home after Liza Minnelli voted them off. They made soup instead of pie, which the judges scooped out with my fingernails, and at the bottom, they found Dr. J and Mr. H bloated with Abuelita and cellophane.

Happy Days/Get Happy

~~I wrote Señor Arctic off too quickly.~~

~~He lectures cryogenics in the cafeteria. I jot down notes.~~

~~"So, it's like dying without dying?"~~

~~He ices over scientific jargon.~~

~~I am composed of dust houses/dozens of quarter stacks/a smattering of you know what.~~

~~They're serving pozole verde today, my favorite.~~

~~Mr. Double-Side knows what I'm thinking.~~

~~With four or forty ice cubes, Señor can slurp soup without screaming.~~

~~Double-Side nestles his cheek into my lifelines.~~

~~I can tell Señor cares. So many people care.~~

~~Señor asks if mania ever eases the dread.~~

~~I wouldn't be here listening if it did.~~

~~He hugs me tenderly enough to break my spine and his snowglobe body.~~

~~When it's whiteout weather, I spotlight that I am still here~~

Ode to Ammit (i.e., Please Devour Me)

you
       stable
              un-
hooked

summon
still

I trace dappled curve
                 -combed outlets
still

      breast cradled   collapse

closest urge

abrupt
seam-stroke

you sense my
      lowering numbers

un-
      stabilized   obsession

come back

          eventually

head-bound   heart-hungry
                          un-
committed

I   you

      think: afterword

Midsommar (2019)[5]

We've ruined this dance before:

the orange pillars, the teeth
rimmed teeth, me in a duct tape
tux, Mr. Double-Side and Dani
dropmouthed, watching my feet
grip carpet like needles in
a pincushion.

As the music discords, we snap

our phones in half. You intervene
to souvenir my skin, ask if I could
mercy-kill my lithium. There's
a locked door somewhere with our
survival seam ripped from the base.

When I sing, carbon monoxide
wafts out, which, according to
Ratman's colleague, Dr.
Ari Aster, makes sense.

---

[5] "This is a riveting biography," Dr. Ratman says. "You would forget your meds, forget you're my obligation. Sticky yourself to gas and suffer. So much vomit. But I mean, that's the reality of things. You'll sicken yourself inside out." If you look closely in each frame, the fringes of a rat are visible. Dr. Ratman confiscates rolls of tape from my apartment and tells me I should stay away from giant mallets ("Like Princess's—stay away from Princess").

to bruce / to my future / bruce

in memory of Carson Thomas Miller, after the poet Stacey Tran

never forget how to be two blocks away

    any farther   around fatal

    when you need to

no locked doors

    as soon as you feel it, share

my severed

my tether

        as soon as you feel it

            as soon as you feel

    i wish i could say

when you are choking

    remember

    as soon as you need to scream

    as soon as you scream

your plunged chest

        soft neck love

        language

    silence this silence

there will be me who says sin

there will be praise

        on a balcony

where we watch rats learn to kiss

        and you ask if the red

                was any good

i am throating a seat cushion

i am paying an oracle to read

                tea leaves

and you chew the dregs

        there is a me that will   miss you

                always

                bottle you genie-style

ask no wishes

        except you stay

                by my side

ring to suffocate me

    i forever audience

body ensembled

      a series of bruising hands

Bipolar Support Group, Part Two

                    YOU:
There's nothing like wholeness. Like okay, maybe I'm not as far off as I thought I was. Or…I guess what I'm trying to say is, a word was thrust at me, stapled to my chest, and all I had to go off of was Dr. Ratman's opinion. Dr. Ratman's treatment process. Sorry, trigger warning. But here, there are more me's. Not that we're all— not that we have identical experiences. But I'm not alone with a stapled chest. I'm not alone in being told to unswallow the pills or talk to my therapist because I'm living my goddamn life. So what if it looks a little bit like hypomania? So what?

THE GROUP hums in agreement.

                    YOU:
Anyways. What I'm trying to say is…it's relieving to not be the only one stuffed with pink cellophane and needles. It's relieving to know Dr. Rat—… to know *he's* wrong. I'm not going to die alone. I'm not going to die. I'm not going. We are not fractured. We are not only bad blood and craters.

(THE GROUP and YOU dismantle plastic chairs, use the legs to manufacture a fortress. YOU call it Headquarters. MR. DOUBLE-SIDE sneaks his way in. DR. RATMAN is explicitly forbidden.)

There's not much more to see here. Do you understand what's going on? The moon propels bright rings, mutes clustered stars and the Rat Signal. A room has been carved out. I can't decrypt sense. It's like touching your cheek and realizing you've been braided into a film reel you don't want to be in. The room teaches you how to torpedo the screen.

Sitting at a Table with Rahul Kohli and Shira Erlichman

Do I have any right to bring them here? I don't/never know what to say. They claim I'm an organ of masks. How do I reply? How do I lie to them? I remind everyone that Dr. Ratman wears a mask, but they think he's different. They ask for something true. I'm on a journey to the center of my war path. Glaring, Flytrap twines all life away. No chance to warn them, no pause before the vomiting, the curdled faces and undergrowth.

I: a geyser of shit, whatever synonyms you prefer for pain. How else do you want me to phrase it? So, I leave myself bare: how I envy my brother for his lack of defect, how as a sometimes-god I do nothing but help myself, how I am in love with the same bane my tías loved, how I often wish to be a latexed hero in a blockbuster, only focused on a safety plan and looking good, which Rahul and Shira emphasize is not entirely impossible. They listen and nod and my hope is silent but cross-fingered.

Steven Grant and I Commiserate Over Our Respective Brain Functions

A man eats the moon, charts the city crater by crater.
He gulps me whole out of fear I might turn new.
The same man solves twenty Rubik's cubes, under-
lines the importance of hugging statues, and we nestle
wrinkled gold after pilling my bones to salt. He directs me:
never say goodbye to an alligator without rolling up
your sleeves first. Forget forgetting and forge on.
Some itch inside us begs for memory and we can't.
Here's a torn brochure with guidelines for cradled bodies.
We might be it.

Manic and/or Semi-Sentient

penduluming an orangeblue
children's swing

brightheated

            i kick my head

here is what a paused television feels

            i kick back

            i kick back

with stasis comes roll
washing machine belly

i picture you
        leg stretched
        pointing

i'm showing   off

meet me to duel the high-noon sun

my converse begin
gluing themselves
to socks

        and the woodchipped storms
        kick back

                we're too tall too orange too throated

                                    here is what a battery pack feels
                                    fullthrottle

you're close but can't

snatch
my waist my
        my windstruck

                                    you jump
                                    and I repeat

                                    you

a chorus of shouts
                not unlike a revved engine

Ode to Travis Willingham

Mr. Double-Side and I snip multiversal
seams and expose a timeline where he avoids
demolition. Which means in a video game,

I untangle deformation and Travis Willingham
pats Double-Side's back until thread trickles out.

Even when we rescue the sick, they find
ways to betray us, Dr. Ratman says. His rat
ears flop with flocked disappointment.

Travis treats us to pie. Out of respect, he links
his mouth, and we allow it, allow his performance
of our endlessness. Our persistence. Our not quite
physical disaster.

He's the closest to reconstructing our cavitied
chemicals without wearing it

down. Without swapping out cellophane
for mirror shards and calling it close enough.
Travis doesn't gawk at half-cheeks or
CVS receipts. Ratman shrieks, *stop
simultaneously swallowing stop stop stop stop stop*

Oh, Travis.
It's never ideal
but sometimes it's just human enough to be magic.

Disrupting time means apologizing,
stitching our splits. Double-Side and I
hug Travis then each other. We trade
voices and Travis's fits best on me.

                                    i hear you
                                    i hear you
                                    i hear you
                                    i hear you
                                    i hear you
                                    i hear you
                                    i hear you
                                    i hear you
                                    i hear you
                                    i hear you
                                    i hear you
                                    i hear you
                                    i hear you
                                    i   you
                                    i   you
                                    i   you
                                    i   you
                                    i   you
                                    i   you
                                    i   you
                                    i   you
                                                you
                                                you
                                                you
                                                you
                                                you
                                                you

                                    YOU

"Great film! Really drew me in. The crazy girl had a few different things woven together to create an experience in the viewer."[6]

And what am I if not your favorite scare tactic?
A writing room's wet dream?
I've already asked—am I capable?
At what point do I snap inside out?
What is this pain worth at the box office?

---

[6] I show this Quora comment from seven years ago to Dr. Ratman. "It's about that movie, *The Roommate*." He's never heard of it. He recommends I forget I've seen anything and to meditate instead. He favorites twenty hour-long sonic healing episodes on my Spotify. I bargain with him. He agrees to a horror movie night if I clear my headspace of external bullshit.

I DON'T KNOW WHEN I'LL EVER STOP TALKING ABOUT THIS. I TRY TO FUCK THE MOON BECAUSE SHE/HE/THEY HAVE TOO MANY FACES. IN THE SKY, I BEG FOR A RESIDENCY CHANGE, BUT TO THEM I AM A CASUAL HOOKUP, SO THEY HURTLE ME HOME, AN ASTEROID. I'M USED TO SMOKING UP FAST. IF I SAFETY-SCISSOR MY LEGS AND SELL MY SOUL AND ATTACK DR. RATMAN IN BROAD DAYLIGHT WHILE MY CAR EXPLODES, DON'T ASK IF I'M MANIC. AND IF I SNAKE AROUND THE COFFEE TABLE IN GRADUAL GRADIENTS OF NOT THERE, DON'T ASK IF YOU NEED TO 911 DR. RATMAN. PLEASE, I WANT TO FIGURE OUT HOW TO LIVE. DR. RATMAN KEEPS KISSING MY FOREHEAD AND SHOVING A GUN IN MY HANDS TELLING ME TO TRY SENSORY MINDFULNESS AND I DON'T KNOW HOW ANYTHING IS SUPPOSED TO SAVE ME. ONCE I ASKED DR. RATMAN IF HE COULD BEAT ME UP LIKE EVERYONE ELSE. HE DOWNLOADED THE EMOODS TRACKER APP ON MY PHONE INSTEAD.

There's a Speech Bubble Over My Head Saying, "Twice as Ill, Twice as Dangerous!"

Two lithium tablets are enough to commit arson:

1. Strike a match against your inner arm.
2. Let it trickle to your fingertips, settle in your nails like wicked currency.
3. Embed another burning in the center of you, at the root of the mania, the meteor showering of yourself.
4. I forgot a step. Before #3, douse
5. yourself in dialectics and takeout boxes and poorly cleaned toilet water.
6. Unrestrained, liquefy. Spare
7. nothing.

Bipolar Support Group, Part ?

(An alternate reality where MR. DOUBLE-SIDE has both cheeks.)

                    DR. RATMAN:
And how does stability settle into you? My diagnosis is you look quite ordinary.

YOU shush RATMAN. A light crinkling pervades the room, like Rice Krispies cereal being milk-boarded. A theory: YOU tiptoe up to DOUBLE-SIDE, bend him down by the lips, and listen.

                    DS:
Was it ever the acid?

                    YOU:
(stroking his cheek) I'm thankful you're still here.

DR. RATMAN hisses and proceeds to fill six prescription pads, the final one a glitter glue and stickered flipbook that ends with "YOU'RE SICK! YOU NEED HELP!" in Pinterest-inspired cursive.

                    DS:
I guess my therapist needs to put on my face. Issues will resurface and become (un)manageable. All the cellophane is a song I hurt to, y'know? I'm never alone, that's the problem and the solution, but still, I don't expect you to stitch your arms to my disappointment.

                        YOU:
If you rip your skin, I rip mine. Loyalty is
sitting in a room full of people who get it and
garbage-bagging the rest. Would you like me to
bolt the doors? If you need to leave, I'll axe it
down. Let's call it quality control.

YOU kiss DOUBLE-SIDE's forehead and nose and
both cheeks.

RATMAN is chanting NO NO NO NO NO NO NO, insists
YOU and DOUBLE-SIDE are not not normal. He hops
up and down, a Kevlar toddler tantrum. Trying to
force YOU and DOUBLE-SIDE apart, RATMAN wiggles
his tail, but YOU suggest he try window-paning—
chew some glass instead.

What Some Might Define as Reverse Psychology

dr. ratman strapped down becomes my patient i say
you have no idea how

long i snap doses into tiny fragments
stuff his gums chalky cheeked
centipede his veins for good
measure

do you feel it do you feel it
no space no control do you feel it
ratman he not me himself me
snapping his thumbs to escape do it
do it doit doitdoitdoit do it he

can't swallow can't stop can't
danger my/him/self why can't
i quite enunciate these his
tears

Ratman Meets Me in an Alleyway

and it's too late it's too late it's too late he's too late he's too he's late
it's late I'm too late it's too much too much it's too much too late he's
scooping me he's taking me home he's too late too rough I'm too much
it's too much much late he's home he's taking me he's late I'm pain he's
late I'm scooped he's too home I'm too late he's asking me he's swallowing
he's gifting he's tongue he's much too late he's kissing me I'm no home no him
it's too late too much too taken no saviors he's too scooped he's swallowing
he's me he's kissed he's closed doors I'm saying it's too late it's too late
it's too much he's saying he knows

Is This What You Mean by Journaling?

Maybe sunlight is the answer to chemical chaos. Planted
in a park beneath high glare and there's not a mood
cycle in sight. Just three shirtless guys huh-ing
over a basketball and cumbía playlists.

                         Most days, I imagine holding Double-Side's hands
                              for hours, as he asks are-you-okay-love? and
                                          why-should-i-hide?
                                      and guarantees he
                        hasn't-given-up-on-my-better-half.
                            I am not enough to materialize.
                                 The DS-ism persists until
              I whisper his name mid-lecture and my students
                        huh their way out of class early.

Is this not a comfortable safeguard?
In the park, I realize
I'm going to marry a woman
(if I ever choose to re-enter the world
as an emotionally complex being). Sorry huh-ing
basketball boys. Sorry synaptic star.
Sorry inner survivalist.

There's so much life I don't want to see.
Or, let's rephrase. Two basketball hoops
taunt each other on opposite ends
of the court. Rivalry. One calls the other cheap rust
to which the insulted replies
that's not what your mom said when she pegged me.
Gateway drugs for mutual attraction
always twister into romance. Doesn't matter how
relentlessly a net unravels, it's never
as long as you're hoping. What's left for the hoops
if not longing unresolved?
A never-union. I don't want to see

but I'm learning a thing or two about choice.
When Dr. Ratman's gone, I decide
who I'm left with. I say, I don't understand
the point of (de)commodifying one's crazy.
If Dr. Ratman swooped in now,
I'd unearth the Double-Side
as an alternative to rat poison,
knot him into my neck where
semi-translucent faces swell
as beckonings
toward a multi-mooned future.

Shoo Ratman, shoo.
I need you and repel you,
a possibly sixty-year-long cycle.

I Dream of Multiverses Without Madness

hate every soft rippled indication
you've curled under my bed ultimate
bogeyman ultimate barrier between me
and superior versions of me

hate your outline in the middle midnight
asphalt your reflection behind me you're raising
gooseflesh garishness gouging out my kidneys

hate that sometimes you're exactly what
scripts sketch you out to be hate your
weaseling between possibility between

a love i skim my stress ball heart my shredded
stability hate how you tear me from intimacy
from a timeline where i could

have said yes kiss me and wouldn't have worried
about highlow breakage cracked composure
flood of greater proportion wouldn't have
whirlpooled puddled wouldn't have drowned
our own chances would have said thank
you for a brain superglued together

hate you composed into me
permanent disordered reprise

hate and hate i am

I SKIN MYSELF AS A LAST RESORT. AUDIENCE, TAKE CARE OF HER. IF INCLINED TO TOSS HER IN A PLASTIC BAG AND DROWN HER IN THE BACKYARD POOL, WAIT. LET HER USE YOU. SHE'LL SLINK TO THE SENSITIVE STENCH OF MY ILLNESS WHEN SHE'S READY.

Bipolar Support Group, Archived

YOU and MR. DOUBLE-SIDE are on a date. He tacks together a bicolored suit and bedazzles his marionette lines. DR. RATMAN gifts YOU a pill-bottled jacket as a token of support. DOUBLE-SIDE picks YOU up at six, drives to a Longhorn Steakhouse. In this steakhouse, no one stares. No one plucks apart your Dents. In this steakhouse, there are no rat signals. No capes. No paws. The server asks how YOU like your coffee. DOUBLE-SIDE talks about the before and YOU encase his hand to sketch out smattered lifelines. The Longhorn Steakhouse DJ spits ultimate mash-ups: Fallout Boy meets Frank Sinatra meets Sting. The DJ is very proud of themselves. On this date, YOU and DOUBLE-SIDE scarf down secret menu cherry pie and lick each other's forks clean.

YOU:
I've never been on a date where I didn't have to hide.

DS:
Me too. I haven't been on a date where someone finds me beautiful, not since the diagnosis.

YOU:
What are we supposed to be here? Are we still the apocalypse? The test tubes and the chalk?

DS:
Your thumb is my thumb and I stroke each of our knuckles. The dream is to enjoy a meal and get you home safe. This steakhouse is just a steakhouse, rat free.

YOU believe DOUBLE-SIDE, marvel at his holographic pink, his curved conviction, the knotting of his fate and his other fate. Skimming his skin is like fucking the moon, so YOU whisper constellation names into his corroded pores. YOU can't resist studying DOUBLE-SIDE, thinking oh Mr. Quarter and Collapse, so charred, so stunning. My favorite form of cracking. DOUBLE-SIDE pays the bill, walks YOU to your door.

                    DS:
Can I kiss you goodnight?

                    YOU:
Yes/no/maybe/only on the cheek. Or maybe come inside instead.

YOU can't mix the meds so YOU are forced to offer water. DR. RATMAN once thought hydration was the missing piece, the final cog in your restoration, and trashed your fridge accordingly. DS understands and refills your Brita.

                    YOU:
Double-Side, do you ever want to die?

                    DS:
Yes, always. (His fingers ghost the mountain range of his jawline.) Every day, in fact.

                    YOU:
I want to die, DS. I want to die and everyone cares.

                    DS(nodding):
And everyone cares.

Nothing scandalous or shocking happens. YOU and DOUBLE-SIDE cocoon, trade your embarrassing histories. You tuck each other's hair behind seared ears. It's as close to normal as you'll get. Tomorrow, DR. RATMAN Returns. Tomorrow, YOU slink back to Asylum jumpsuits and committing crimes. Back to wellness checks. Neither of you think about that now. You gently kiss. Savor your moment. Enjoy someone who knows.

No eyes on YOU. Just two people cross-fingered and hopeful.

NOTES

"FOR YOUR DYING PLEASURE, WE'RE SERVING THE VERY SAME ACID THAT MADE US [WHO] WE ARE" is a quote from Joel Schumacher's *Batman Forever* (1995).

The title **MAD LOVE (1993 & 1995)** is a reference to an episode of The New Batman Adventures (1993) that details Harley Quinn's backstory, her love for the Joker, and their unhealthy relationship dynamics. It's also a reference to the drama/romance movie starring Drew Barrymore (1995), in which her character purportedly has bipolar disorder.

A WELLNESS CHECK: The lines starting with "Located in G. City…" and "Amadeus decided, as sole heir…" are borrowed from the Wikipedia entry on Arkham Asylum. The quote "those who are considered to no longer be mentally unwell tend to re-offend" is from the Wikipedia entry on Arkham Asylum. The quote "… too psychologically paralyzing for anyone to thrive?" is from the American Psychiatric Association's (APA) web post "What Are Bipolar Disorders?" on Psychiatry.org.

ON BEING IN LOVE WITH THE CLOWN PRINCESS OF CRIME: The first, third, fifth, and final stanzas refer to WebMD, Mayo Clinic, and APA entries on Histrionic Personality Disorder, Schizotypal Personality Disorder, and Bipolar Disorder, as well as treatments for all three conditions.

HYPOMANIC? ABSOLUTELY. BUT OH, SO DIVINE! is a reference to the 2005 New York Times article "Hypomanic? Absolutely. But Oh, So Productive," written by Benedict Carey.

IN WHICH I (FINALLY) AM NOT REAL: the text is an erasure poem of Gin Mahli et al.'s article, "Bipolar II Disorder Is a Myth," published in the Canadian Journal of Psychiatry in 2019.

The title of **I'M NOT TRYING TO BE MUCH OF A PERSON RIGHT NOW** is a lyric from Mook's song "Malmo." Paul Dano is the lead singer of this band.

The poem **MIDSOMMAR (2019)** is named after a horror movie written and directed by Ari Aster. The film opens with the main character—Dani Ardor—trying to get into contact with her sister, Terri. Dani's sister, however, has murdered her parents and committed suicide by filling their home with carbon monoxide. Terri duct tapes a tube that runs from the family's car directly to her face. Prior to the incident, it's revealed that Terri has bipolar disorder.

Steven Grant in **STEVEN GRANT AND I COMMISERATE OVER OUR RESPECTIVE BRAIN FUNCTIONS** is from Marvel Comics' and the Marvel Cinematic Universe. His alter-ego is Moon Knight. Steven Grant canonically has Dissociative Identity Disorder.

ODE TO TRAVIS WILLINGHAM references voice actor Travis Willingham who plays Harvey Dent in Batman: The Telltale Series. In this video game, the player can choose to save Harvey Dent from a falling stagelight, preventing his facial scarring. Dent, however, still becomes Two-Face during a mental breakdown.

The title **"GREAT FILM! REALLY DREW ME IN. THE CRAZY GIRL HAD A FEW DIFFERENT THINGS WOVEN TOGETHER TO CREATE AN EXPERIENCE IN THE VIEWER"** is from a Quora comment by Sean Halle, posted in 2015. His comment responded to a question about The Roommate (2011), a thriller horror movie in which the antagonist is an obsessive college student with mental illness. Sean's reply is extensive, breaking down what illness this character may have. He only refers to her as "crazy girl." Wikipedia says she may have schizophrenia or bipolar disorder.

"THERE'S A SPEECH BUBBLE OVER MY HEAD SAYING, 'TWICE AS ILL, TWICE AS DANGEROUS!'" is in reference to DC Comics's 234th issue of Batman with Robin the Teen Wonder, titled "The Return of Two-Face: Twice as Evil—Twice as Dangerous," published in 1971.

ACKNOWLEDGEMENTS

Many thanks to the editors of the following publications in which these poems, sometimes in earlier drafts, first appeared:

Neuro Magazine: "< ? >" (pg. 17)

Substantially Unlimited: "Ratman Streams My Diagnosis on Netflix" (formerly "Stream My Diagnosis on Netflix") and "*Mad Love* (1993 & 1995)"

Janus Literary: "*Midsommar* (2019)," pg. 45, formerly titled "On Arkham Asylum's Screening Process," "Dual Form Insanity (You're Thinking, How Much More Is There To Say?)," "In Which I Am (Finally) Not Real," "Steven Grant and I Commiserate Over Our Respective Brain Functions"

Bear Creek Gazette: "Scene from a Bipolar Support Group, Part One"

bloodbathhate: "Ratman and I Refill Our Prescriptions"

Juke Joint: "< ¿ >"

ERGI Press: "Hypomanic? Absolutely. But Oh, So Divine!" in *Trickster: An Anthology of Queer Mischief*

GRATITUDES

Thank you to Josh Savory, MJ Malpiedi, Ally Ang, and everyone on the Game Over Books team for giving my work a home, for treating Ratman with care and consideration, for believing in me and my writing. You nerds are my absolute favorite.

Thank you to my incredible mentors, professors, and role models: Jessica Q. Stark, who inspires me to chase my obsessions and flesh them out, who I am incredibly in awe of. Thank you for reading Ratman in its roughest stages and encouraging me to write about him. Noah Eli Gordon, my first MFA workshop professor, who supported my crazy and monstrous, who I miss with every poem I write. Thank you to Ben Robertson, Cecily Parks, Julie Weng, and Stephen Harmon. Vi Khi Nao, whose workshop sparked this collection. To Megan Cobb and Johna Adams. To Shira Erlichman, whose book, *Odes to Lithium*, reassured me that writing about mental illness, and bipolar disorder specifically, is not only allowed, but much needed.

Thank you to Stacy Gerberich for helping me manage the impossibility of existence. Thank you for accepting all my multitudes and helping me heal them.

To my friends and found family: Delaney Dunn, Joe Gonzalez, Masky, Bethany Wilcox, Lillian Bautista, Mon Sato, Nik Calo, Kayla Sanchez, thank you for your endless compassion and friendship. To Elva Patino, thank you for being my biggest fan since day one, back when I was writing *Austin & Ally* fanfics in middle school. Y'all's wildness is infectious and lovely. Smooches for you all.

To my cohort—though we be few, man are we absolutely groundbreaking. Brian Fortune, Isabel Phelps, and Lilly Rothman, thank y'all for your excitement and critiques and cheers. Y'all are true gems. And to Beau Farris: you put so much faith and support into me as a writer—you're a supreme hype man.

To my parents, thank y'all for encouraging me to explore writing. Marisa, my sweet sibling, I'd be incomplete without our laughter, rage, tears, love, hatred, and vigilance. A piece of you exists in this collection.

Chris Soliz and Dane Stull, two of my favorite writers, thank you for being pillars of inspiration, for supporting me without hesitation. Conspiring against our own D&D characters' well-being is my favorite pastime. I'm so lucky to have learned what creation means from you both. Quincey, thank you for calling, texting, FaceTiming me the instant I admit my brain is vacuuming me into its black-hole center. For always loving (and roasting) me, even when I make it a challenge.

Anjali Ravi and JP Mayer. You both, of all people, said hell yeah, write about *The Batman*. Make him a rat. Make him whatever you need him to be. Thank you for the time and belief you put into my work. Every day I'm more and more thankful for our weird, chaotic insanities. Gods bless y'all two. I, the largest vessel of love for y'all.

I struggle with expressing sentiments beyond humor and anger. If your name isn't listed here, or you read these acknowledgements and find them reaching but not quite captivating our history, just know I love you all dearly. I'll never be able to encapsulate the gratitude I have. I often say being a person is shitty and difficult business. With all of you, being a person is worth it.

And to YOU, reader, thank you for leaping into the world of Ratman. Thank you for giving this book a chance.

Biography

Bri Gonzalez is a queer, Chicane poet from San Antonio, Texas. More of Bri's work can be found or forthcoming in Honey Literary, Crow & Cross Keys, Angel Rust, Talon Review, ERGI Press' Trickster: An Anthology of Queer Mischief, Devil's Party Press' Solstice: A Winter Anthology, and others. Bri is a graduate of the Summer '23 Napa Valley Writers' Conference and will receive their MFA in Creative Writing from the University of Colorado Boulder in Spring 2024. In their free time, they smother their void cat, Dahlia, play excessive amounts of D&D, and swoon over fictional characters. Check Bri out at bgwriting.org.